D0456775

WHAT IS THIS?

a. mold growing on some really old leftovers

b. an image from a brain scan

c. a satellite image that led explorers to a lost city

C.

It's an image taken by satellite to help explorers locate a lost city.

In the 1990s, an archeologist convinced NASA, the U.S. space agency, to have one of its satellites take high-tech images of a remote desert. He suspected that the mysterious, ancient city of Ubar had been located there.

When the archeologist saw the photos, he was amazed. But would these images help him locate Ubar? Read on to find out.

Book design Red Herring Design/NYC
Supervising editor: Jeffrey Nelson

Library of Congress Cataloging-in-Publication Data
Rinaldo, Denise.
Cities of the dead : finding lost civilizations / by Denise Rinaldo.
p. cm. — (24/7 : science behind the scenes)
Includes bibliographical references and index.
ISBN-13: 978-0-531-12079-8 (lib. bdg.)   978-0-531-18739-5 (pbk.)
ISBN-10: 0-531-12079-1 (lib. bdg.)   0-531-18739-X (pbk.)
1. Civilization, Ancient—Juvenile literature. 2. Lost
continents—Juvenile literature. 3. Extinct cities—Juvenile
literature. 4. Antiquities—Juvenile literature. 5. Excavations
(Archaeology)—Juvenile literature. 6. Archaeology—Field
work—Juvenile literature. I. Title.
CB311.R565 2007
930.1—dc22   2006021239

CITIES
OF THE
DEAD

Finding Lost Civilizations

Denise Rinaldo

WARNING: Some civilizations die. Cities are destroyed by flood or fire. They're buried by lava, or they sink into the sea. And then the world forgets about them. If stories about people vanishing off the face of the earth give you the creeps, this book is not for you.

Franklin Watts®
An Imprint of Scholastic Inc.
New York • Toronto • London • Auckland • Sydney
Mexico City • New Delhi • Hong Kong
Danbury, Connecticut

CONTENTS

TRUE-LIFE CASE FILES!

Follow the search for three lost civilizations.

A desert in Oman covers a mystery.

15 Case #1: Ancient Ubar: Lost City of Arabia

There are legends about a rich city that sank beneath the sands of the Arabian desert. Are these old tales true?

27 Case #2: Atlantis: Island of Dreams

Was there once a beautiful island civilization known as Atlantis—or was it just a philosopher's fantasy?

Could Atlantis be here, near the Rock of Gibraltar?

This island in the Pacific is home to huge, mysterious statues.

35 Case #3: Easter Island: Secrets of the Statues

Giant stone figures stand along the shore of this remote island. Who built them—and why?

Want to dig deeper? Here's more information about archeologists and their discoveries.

A story tells of a fantastic ancient culture. The tale is passed down from generation to generation. Is it a legend— or the truth?

LOST CIVILIZATIONS 411

Mysterious statues are found. Who made them—and for what reason?

Solving puzzles like these is a job for an archeologist.

IN THIS SECTION:

- ▶ how archeologists really talk;
- ▶ the world's most famous lost civilizations;
- ▶ who works with archeologists to solve ancient mysteries.

Can You Dig It?

Archeologists have their own way of talking. Find out what their vocabulary means.

legend (LEJ-uhnd) a story passed down from earlier times that has not been proven to be true

Let's plan an expedition to find out whether the civilization existed, or if it is just a **legend**.

Soon we'll be **excavating** on a sunny island in the Pacific!

excavating (EK-skuh-vay-ting) digging up and recovering artifacts and other clues about people of the past

> We think these coins may be **artifacts** of a lost **civilization**.

artifacts
(ART-uh-fakts) objects made by humans, especially tools or weapons used in the past

civilization
(siv-ih-luh-ZAY-shuhn) a highly developed and organized society with its own culture and technology

> That's what I love about **archeology**. You get to explore so many great places.

archeology
(ar-kee-OL-uh-jee) the study of past cultures. Archeologists study buildings, graves, objects, human remains, and artifacts.

> Sorry, but the **evidence** points in the direction of snowy Siberia.

evidence
(EV-uh-duhnss) information or facts used to prove something

Say What?

Here's some other lingo an archeologist might use on the job.

date
(dayt) to determine the age of an artifact
*"Archeologists sometimes use chemical tests to **date** objects found at ruins."*

dig
(dig) in archeology, a dig is a site that is being excavated—or dug up
*"I worked on a **dig** in the Sahara Desert. It was so hot I didn't think I'd survive."*

fieldwork
(FEELD-wurk) work done at a dig or other archeological site
*"She had studied all the maps and read all the ancient legends. Now she needed to do some **fieldwork**."*

sediment
(SED-uh-muhnt) solid stuff that has been carried by water
*"Months after the flood, we found tiny bits of pottery in the **sediment**."*

Lost and Found

For centuries, people didn't know whether these lost cities had ever existed. And then archeologists unearthed them.

LOST: The City of Troy

According to an ancient legend, a city called Troy was destroyed during the Trojan War, a ten-year conflict with the Greeks.

The Trojan War began after Paris, a young man from Troy, visited Greece and fell in love with the beautiful Helen. Helen was already married—to a Greek king—but she went with Paris to Troy.

Enraged, Helen's husband gathered 100,000 soldiers and 1,000 ships to conquer Troy and bring Helen home. Eventually, the Greeks destroyed Troy by sneaking soldiers into the city inside a giant wooden horse.

The ancient Greek author Homer composed a work called *The Iliad*

The Greeks supposedly used a trick defeat Troy. They gave the city a gif huge wooden horse. But it turned o be packed with Greek soldiers.

about these events. But did Tr ever really exist?

FOUND: In modern-day Tu

In 1871, a man named Hein Schliemann found the ruins of Archeologists later discovered nine cities had been built on t same site over 2,500 years. T seventh one dates from aroun 1200 BC. That's when the Troj War would have taken place. A the ruins show that the city re *was* destroyed in a war.

A fan of *The Iliad*, Heinrich Schliem began uncovering the ruins of Troy

The ancient city of Pompeii was perfectly preserved under a layer of volcanic ash.

LOST: The City of Pompeii

Pompeii was a busy seaside city in the Roman Empire. Rich people from Rome spent their summers there. They filled their beautiful houses with artwork and other treasures. But in AD 79, a volcano called Mount Vesuvius buried Pompeii under a thick blanket of ash. Centuries passed, and most people forgot about the city.

FOUND: In modern-day Italy

Throughout history, farmers living near Mount Vesuvius found artifacts that seemed to have come from Pompeii. In 1748, archeologists began to excavate.

The volcanic ash preserved many of the buildings and objects. They're almost exactly like they were on the day of the eruption. Today, you can visit Italy, walk the streets of Pompeii, and get a feel for what life was like there.

LOST: The City of Vilcabamba

From about AD 1200 to 1572, the Inca Empire controlled most of western South America. It was an advanced culture, with a strong government, an elaborate system of roads, beautiful art and architecture, and excellent medical care.

Starting in 1532, Francisco Pizarro of Spain conquered much of the Inca Empire. But a leader called Manco Inca and thousands of his followers fled to a mountain city called Vilcabamba. From there, they continued to fight the Spaniards for about 30 years.

In 1911, American explorer Hiram Bingham set off to search for Vilcabamba in the high mountains of Peru.

FOUND: Machu Picchu, in modern-day Peru

Bingham made one of the greatest archeological finds of the last century. He stumbled upon Machu Picchu, a mountaintop city of temples and palaces. (It was so lost nobody was even looking for it.) Bingham later discovered the ruins of Vilcabamba, but they were not nearly as spectacular as Machu Picchu.

The Inca city of Machu Picchu is the most visited tourist site in Peru.

The Archeology Team

Here's a look at some of the people who search for and study lost civilizations.

LAB TECHNICIANS

They conduct scientific tests to answer questions about each artifact found at a dig. For example: How old is it? Who made it? Where is it from?

ARCHEOLOGISTS

Archeologists research the possible location of a lost city. Once the site is located, the head archeologist directs the team at the dig.

HISTORIANS

They provide information about the history of the ancient civilization and help figure out whether legends have any basis in fact.

LOST CITIES

These are cities that were part of civilizations that no longer exist. Usually, there are legends, writings, or artifacts that give clues about lost cities.

ARCHEOLOGICAL DIVERS

They help collect evidence from archeological sites located under water.

ARCHEOLOGY STUDENTS

College students conduct research under the direction of an archeologist or history professor and often help at the dig.

FIELD CREW MEMBERS

Some workers specialize in unearthing evidence without causing damage. Others keep a good photographic record of the evidence.

TRUE-LIFE CASE FILES!

24 hours a day, 7 days a week, 365 days a year, archeologists are solving mysteries from the past.

IN THIS SECTION:

▶ archeologists use satellites to help track down an ancient city;

▶ tiny pollen fossils reveal the cause of a civilization's downfall;

▶ scientists look for the lost city of Atlantis.

Gridding a Site

A volunteer at a dig in England copies the grid on the ground onto graph paper.

Here's how archeologists keep a record of what they find on a dig.

What does an archeologist do first when she gets to a dig site? She turns the site into a grid that looks sort of like a giant piece of graph paper. Archeologists call this "gridding a site."

The archeologist creates a grid of equal-sized squares on the ground. Then she gives each square its own number.

Next, she copies this grid onto a piece of graph paper. Each tiny square on the paper represents a square on the ground.

When the archeologist finds an artifact, she labels it with the number of the square in which it was found. She also goes to her graph paper and makes a note showing where this artifact was found.

Later, the archeologist can consult her graph paper and know exactly which artifact was found where. Also, archeologists in the future can consult these grids to review the history of the dig.

An archeologist grids a site on Easter Island. She measures each square carefully and uses string and wooden stakes to create the grid.

Rub' al-Khali Desert,
1990s

Ancient Ubar:
Lost City of Arabia

There are legends about a
rich city that sank beneath the
sands of the Arabian desert.
Are these old tales true?

15

The Road to Ubar

An explorer comes across a path in the desert. Could it lead to a legendary lost city?

The year is 1930. Bertram Thomas, a British explorer, has been trekking for days through the vast Rub' al-Khali desert, in southern Arabia. "Look!" says Thomas's guide. He is pointing to a wide path in the sand. "There's the road to Ubar!"

Thomas knew the legend: The rich, beautiful trading city had been built by a powerful king. He wanted it to be a paradise on Earth. It became the world's largest supplier of **frankincense**, a kind of incense made from the sap of a local tree. Frankincense was used in perfume, medicine, and **embalming**—preserving dead bodies. In the ancient world, frankincense was as valuable as gold.

Many ancient civilizations used sap from the frankincense tree to create a highly valued type of incense.

Bertram Thomas (*center*) was the first European to cross the Rub' al-Khali desert. Some of its sand dunes are almost 1,000 feet (300 m) tall. Here, Thomas stands with a group of armed warriors.

In the 1990s, a filmmaker, an explorer, and an archeologist traveled to the Rub' al-Khali desert in the Arabian peninsula to look for the lost city of Ubar.

According to the legend, the people of Ubar became wealthy from their trade in frankincense. They also became greedy and filled with pride. It was said that God became so angry with them that he made the city vanish beneath the sands.

Thomas didn't turn down the path that day. He was running low on water. And the goal of his journey was to become the first European to cross the Rub' al-Khali desert. He might not make it if he went chasing after a legend.

Still, he took careful notes about the location of the road his guide had shown him.

A Modern Searcher

Nicholas Clapp decides that Ubar is not just a legend. And he wants NASA to help him find it.

Flash forward to California in the 1980s. Nicholas Clapp, a filmmaker and amateur archeologist, had become **obsessed** with Ubar.

Clapp had read everything he could about the legendary city. He first learned about it in an old book of stories called *The Book of the One Thousand and One Nights*. He read about the city in writings from ancient Rome. He also learned that it is mentioned in the Koran, the Muslim holy book.

Clapp devoured Thomas's story about the road to Ubar. He pored over ancient maps. And he became convinced that Ubar was real.

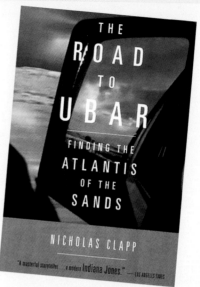

Nicholas Clapp, an amateur archeologist, was obsessed with the stories about Ubar. He convinced NASA to help him search for the lost city. Then he wrote this book, *The Road to Ubar: Finding the Atlantis of the Sands.*

Clapp decided to plan an expedition to find the lost city. But the Rub' al-Khali desert is huge—the size of Texas. How could he narrow his search?

He decided to call NASA. That's right, NASA, the National Aeronautics and Space Administration—the U.S. space agency.

"I'd like to talk to someone about using the space shuttle to find a lost city," Clapp said to the NASA phone operator.

What was he thinking?

NASA's mission is to explore space. But it also studies Earth from space. Scientists use spacecraft equipped with high-tech cameras to take photos of the planet. And some of NASA's imaging technology can actually see through sand.

When Clapp told NASA scientists about Ubar, they were fascinated—and they wanted to help. As one researcher said to Clapp, "What's science for, if not to find out what exists or doesn't?" So NASA researchers took photos from space of the Rub' al-Khali desert. Then they searched the images for evidence of Ubar.

These images didn't show signs of a lost city in the desert. But they did show a wide, ancient road under the sand. Maybe it was the road to Ubar, covered by drifting sands!

MAKING TRACKS

Finding lost roads could be the key to finding the lost city.

Scientists searched for Ubar by looking for roads—especially old buried roads. Why?

Ubar was said to be the center of the frankincense trade. That means that **caravans** of traders would have ridden into the city on camels to buy the frankincense. Then they would have fanned out through the ancient world to sell the precious product.

This constant trekking would have created roads across the desert. And even though they hadn't been used for a long time, these roads might have left permanent marks on the earth.

If scientists could find where all these roads met, perhaps they could locate Ubar.

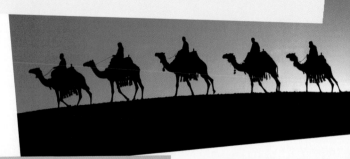

Traders followed roads in and out of Ubar. Could explorers find those ancient roads?

Off to Oman

Using ancient wisdom and modern technology, Clapp starts to zero in on Ubar's possible location.

Now Clapp had enough evidence to convince experienced explorers and archeologists to join an expedition. He put together a team that included Juris Zarins, an archeology professor with years of experience in the Arabian desert. He also recruited Sir Ranulph Fiennes, a man described by the *Guinness Book of World Records* as the world's greatest living explorer.

Using ancient documents, plus the NASA information, the team chose five places to search. All were in Oman—a desert nation on the Arabian **peninsula**. In the summer of 1990, the team traveled to the desert. The search had begun.

Clapp's team spent two weeks in the **scorching** Rub' al-Khali desert. They decided to skip one of the five hot spots they'd identified. It was near a tiny town called Shisur. They thought it was an unlikely spot for a major trading center.

Clapp planned an expedition to the desert of Rub' al-Khali (*above*), in the nation of Oman. He recruited the famous explorer Sir Ranulph Fiennes (*below*).

So where *was* Ubar? The team left Oman without an answer. But they planned to return a few months later to resume the search.

A short time later, though, war broke out in the region. The explorers had to postpone their return to Oman.

But as the war raged, the team received new images from NASA—and those images totally changed their strategy.

Like Spokes on a Wheel

Could the latest images from space lead the searchers to Ubar?

The NASA images were amazing. They showed ancient roads buried beneath the Rub' al-Khali desert. They came from different directions and met at one center point, like spokes on a wheel.

Clapp imagined long camel trains of traders traveling along the spokes and meeting up at a great trading center—Ubar!

In 1991, the war in the area finally came to an end. This time, Clapp's team headed straight for the spot where the roads in the NASA images came together—Shisur. That was the tiny desert village that the team had decided not to visit during their first trip.

When Clapp arrived in Shisur, he asked an elder there if he knew where Ubar was. The man said he didn't. But he added, "maybe not far away." Then he pointed to a spot

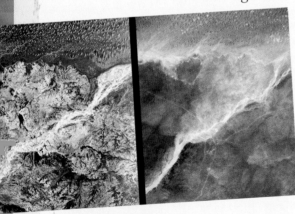

Images of the Rub' al-Khali, taken from the space shuttle. In the radar image at left, some of the ancient roads leading to Ubar show up as red tracks. The roads can be seen more clearly as white lines in the enhanced photo at right.

Left: Archeologists excavate the ancient city of Ubar in the Rub' al-Khali desert. *Below:* The team used a radar device like this one to discover the ruins beneath the sand.

in the distance. There are some ruins there, he told Clapp. But they were not Ubar. They were the remains of a 500-year-old fort.

Ubar, if it existed, disappeared around AD 300. It would be thousands of years old—not hundreds.

Still, the team decided to investigate the ruins. They had brought along an incredible tool they called the red sled. A red sled is a radar device designed to detect things underground. (Radar is a technology used to locate objects by bouncing radio waves off them.) By dragging the red sled across the ground, team members were able to get a rough picture of what lay beneath.

Amazing Finds

A hidden city emerges from the sand. Could it be Ubar?

Thirty feet (9 m) below the surface, the sled detected what looked like a stone well. That was interesting, but what did it mean?

There was just one way to find out. Dig!

Some of Professor Zarins's students flew in to help. Within days, pieces of broken pottery had been found. They were thousands of years old. Some were from pots made in distant lands—like Syria and Greece. This meant that the team had found the home of an ancient people who traded with foreigners. *Like the people of Ubar.*

Professor Juris Zarins (*standing*) and his students from Missouri State University discovered pottery made in ancient Syria and Greece. This was evidence that the ruins were once a great trading city.

Next, the diggers uncovered a wall, then a tower. Soon, the outline of an eight-sided **fortress** was revealed. A 30-foot (9-m) tower had stood at each corner. The fortress had enclosed a small city. Searching inside the walls, team members found unusual artifacts: tools used to turn tree sap into frankincense. *And Ubar was famous for frankincense.*

"The pieces were fitting," Clapp later told *People* magazine. "But we didn't want to jump up and down and shout, 'Ubar! Ubar!' We were afraid we might break the spell."

Case Closed?

If it looks like a lost city and smells like a lost city, is it a lost city?

Had the team found Ubar? Almost certainly. The evidence is amazing. The layout of the walled city matches the legends. And the site dates from the time that Ubar would have existed.

The archeologists also found evidence of the trade caravans that traveled to and from Ubar. They discovered the buried remains of campfires at hundreds of sites around the city. These campfires marked the places where traders pitched their tents for a night of rest before heading back out across the desert.

Even the way the city disappeared echoes the ancient legends. It turned out that Ubar really had sunk into the earth. The excavation revealed

This illustration shows what Ubar might have looked like. Archeologists discovered that the city was a walled fortress with 30-foot (9-m) towers at each corner.

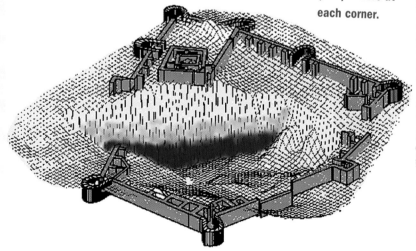

Nicholas Clapp's team excavated these ancient walls that were once part of the city of Ubar.

a huge limestone cavern under the walled city. Scientists think the city was destroyed when it collapsed into the cavern.

After thousands of years, the legendary city had finally been found. NASA's technology had helped solve the ancient mystery. But the success of the mission was due to something much more basic, according to Professor Zarins: "Brains!" By putting their brains together to make sense of evidence from a huge variety of sources, the team members had made a historic discovery. **24/7**

In the next case, read about a legendary paradise that has been the inspiration for beach resorts, animated movies—and serious explorers.

Atlantis: Island of Dreams

Was there once a beautiful island civilization known as Atlantis—or was it just a philosopher's fantasy?

Lost Forever?

According to a famous Greek philosopher, this island was paradise.

Atlantis was said to be a beautiful city with fountains, exotic animals, and stunning architecture.

Imagine a city where gold and silver temples rise high into the sky. Fantastic fountains spout hot and cold water. Tame elephants roam the streets. The king is fair and powerful. He controls a navy strong enough to conquer neighboring lands.

This amazing city is Atlantis, the most famous lost civilization ever.

Atlantis was first described by Plato, a famous Greek **philosopher**. In a book written around 360 BC, he described it in detail.

He said that Atlantis was a fantastic island kingdom that had existed thousands of years before his time. (Unlike Disney's Atlantis, Plato's was not underwater.)

The island was round. It was built in the form of **concentric** rings. (Concentric refers to a circle inside a circle.) Plato described Atlantis as a series of rings within rings. And all these rings were connected by bridges and canals.

But *where* was this island? Plato said it was located "in front of the Pillars of Hercules." Plato's readers would have known that according to Greek myths, these pillars were formed when the Greek hero Hercules split a mountain in two.

Plato gave only one other clue about the island's location. He said that it "was the way to other islands, and from these you might pass to the whole of the opposite continent."

So what had happened to this beautiful kingdom? According to Plato, the citizens of Atlantis became **corrupt** and mean, and the gods decided to punish them. They sent a huge earthquake to shake the island. The earthquake created a **tsunami**, and mountain-sized waves swept over the island. Atlantis was swallowed up by the sea.

Was Plato's story true? This great thinker was known to write about events that had really happened. But he also wrote **allegories**—fictional stories meant to teach lessons.

So which was the story of Atlantis—fact or allegory?

That's a question archeologists, scholars, and treasure-hunters are still trying to answer.

Plato (*in red robe*) was the first person to write about Atlantis. Here, he talks with his student, Aristotle (*in blue*), another Greek philosopher.

Plato wrote that Atlantis was made up of concentric rings, as shown here.

29

ALL OVER THE MAP

People have been searching for Atlantis ever since Plato wrote about it. This map pinpoints some recent searches.

UNITED KINGDOM

IRELAND

ATLANTIC OCEAN

SPAIN

Strait of Gibraltar

MED.

Cuba (2002)
George Erikson, an American anthropologist, thinks there's an underwater city off the coast of Cuba. He believes it's Atlantis.

CUBA

Spartel Island, in the Strait of Gibraltar (2003)
French geographer Jacques Collina-Girard believes this sunken island is exactly where Plato said Atlantis was located.

BOLIVIA

PACIFIC OCEAN

Bolivia (1997–2002)
British explorer Colonel John Blashford-Snell searches for Atlantis in Bolivia. He says that satellite mapping of the bottom of a lake here shows the ruins of canals like the ones Plato described.

Ireland (2004)

Ulf Erlingsson, a Swedish geographer, believes that Atlantis was fictional. But he claims that Plato based the descriptions of its geography on Ireland.

Land's End (1997)

A team of Russian historians search 100 miles (161 km) off the southwest coast of England. They say the location matches Plato's description.

Marisma de Hinojos (2004)

German physicist Rainer Kühne says that satellite photos of this area in Spain show ruins under a salt marsh that match Plato's temples.

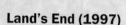

CYPRUS SYRIA

Mediterranean Sea, between Cyprus and Syria (2004)

American researcher Robert Sarmast studies images of the ocean floor here. Sarmast says that these images show walls and hills similar in size and shape to those described by Plato.

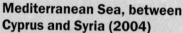

INDONESIA

INDIAN OCEAN

Indonesia (2002)

One of the islands of Indonesia is actually Atlantis, says computer scientist Zia Abbas. He claims that Plato's tale matches old Indonesian legends.

This Just In . . .

A French researcher finds a sunken island—at the very spot where Plato had said that Atlantis was located.

The Strait of Gibraltar, as seen from the space shuttle. This channel of water separates Europe (top land mass) and Africa (bottom land mass).

The giant Rock of Gibraltar is on the north side of the strait.

If Atlantis *did* exist, where was it? In the 2,000 years since Plato wrote about it, people have come up many different theories about its location.

One of the most recent was developed by a French researcher named Jacques Collina-Girard. He says he knows where Atlantis is. And he claims that his theory has something going for it that others don't: It closely matches Plato's descriptions.

Collina-Girard is an expert in geography and ancient history. Part of his work involves figuring out how humans moved from Europe to Africa during the last ice age—about 11,000 years ago.

In the early 2000s, this respected researcher also found himself searching for Atlantis.

It all began when Collina-Girard's studies took him to the Strait of Gibraltar. That's the narrow channel of water that separates Spain (in Europe) from Morocco (in Africa). It's also the gateway between the Atlantic Ocean and the Mediterranean Sea.

Historians believe that in Plato's time, this gateway was known as the Pillars of Hercules. That's because of the giant rocks and cliffs on either side of the channel.

And Plato had written that Atlantis was near the Pillars of Hercules!

Plato had also written that the island linked two continents. Collina-Girard thought that was a valuable clue. Why?

Collina-Girard had done a lot of research on this area. And he had started to believe that there might have once been a land bridge across the strait. Ancient people could have walked across it from Europe to Africa.

To test his theory, Collina-Girard decided to examine the ocean floor of the Strait of Gibraltar for traces of that land bridge. Amazingly, he found a cluster of undersea islands.

Collina-Girard calculated that the last of these islands disappeared underwater about 11,000 years ago. That's when the ice age ended. Huge amounts of ice melted, and the sea levels rose. This would have made the island disappear.

French researcher Jacques Collina-Girard believes that Atlantis could have been what is now called Spartel Island. This island is now underwater. But 19,000 years ago, it was above sea level.

And according to Plato, Atlantis disappeared about 11,000 years ago!

Collina-Girard became convinced. Spartel Island, the last island to disappear underwater, was Atlantis.

SPAIN

Gibraltar

Strait of Gibraltar

Spartel Island

Atlantic Ocean

Mediterranean Sea

MOROCCO

Teaming Up

Collina-Girard joins forces with an undersea explorer.

In 2003, Collina-Girard gave a speech about his findings in the Strait of Gibraltar at an archeology conference. Paul-Henri Nargeolet, an undersea explorer, was in the audience.

During the 1990s, Nargeolet had used a small submarine called a **submersible** to explore the *Titanic*. He suggested that he and Collina-Girard use one to investigate Spartel Island, which is 320 feet (98 m) below sea level.

The two explorers don't expect to find the fancy temples and luxurious buildings often associated with Atlantis. "Those are dreams," Nargeolet told the British Broadcasting Service. Instead, they expect to find crumbled walls, tools, and weapons.

Will Collina-Girard and Nargeolet discover artifacts that prove that Spartel Island really is Atlantis? The expedition is still in the planning stages. But someday soon, Collina-Girard and Nargeolet's submersible will surface with the facts. Will the headlines say, "Atlantis Found!" or "Atlantis Still Lost!"? Stay tuned. 24/7

Explorer Paul-Henri Nargeolet was convinced by Collina-Girard's theory about the location of Atlantis. "I couldn't believe no one had drawn this conclusion before," he said. He's seen here with Millvina Dean, a survivor from the *Titanic*; he had explored that wreck in his submersible.

In the next case, find out about a tiny island in the Pacific Ocean that is home to hundreds of stony-faced giants.

Easter Island, a
Chilean Island in the
Pacific Ocean
1722-present

Easter Island: Secrets of the Statues

Giant stone figures stand along
the shore of this remote island.
Who built them—and why?

A Surprising Sight

A sea captain comes across an island populated by giants.

On Easter morning in 1722, Admiral Jacob Roggeveen, a Dutch sea captain, stood at the **helm** of his ship and watched as a tiny island came into view. Roggeveen had been at sea for nearly eight months, exploring remote parts of the Pacific Ocean. He had not expected to run across this slip of land. And when Roggeveen saw the island up close, he was truly "struck with astonishment," he wrote in his journal.

The coast was lined with gigantic stone statues.

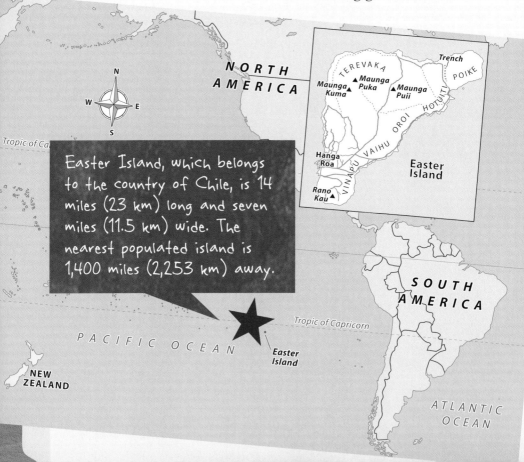

NORTH AMERICA

N W E S

Tropic of Ca

Easter Island, which belongs to the country of Chile, is 14 miles (23 km) long and seven miles (11.5 km) wide. The nearest populated island is 1,400 miles (2,253 km) away.

TEREVAKA
Maunga Kuma ▲ Maunga Puka
Maunga Puii ▲
Trench
POIKE
OROI
HOTUITI
VAIHU
Hanga Roa
VINAPU
Rano Kau ▲
Easter Island

PACIFIC OCEAN

Easter Island

Tropic of Capricorn

NEW ZEALAND

SOUTH AMERICA

ATLANTIC OCEAN

They were human in form, and many of them stood on carefully carved platforms. Some had huge red blocks on their heads. Most of them had their backs to the sea. Their huge eyes gazed at the island's bare landscape.

These statues must have been built by an advanced society, Roggeveen thought. He expected to find a well-organized community when he landed on the island. But he was in for a shock.

Captain James Cook, a British explorer, was the second westerner to visit Easter Island. He's shown here examining a statue in 1774.

The Mystery Deepens
Roggeveen goes ashore and is puzzled by what he sees.

When Roggeveen and his men went ashore, they found a community of about 2,000 people. They had a few leaky canoes, and not much else. Except for some chickens, there were no animals larger than insects. The island had no trees or bushes taller than 10 feet (3 m). And nobody was carving statues.

"The island's wasted appearance could give no other impression than of a singular poverty and

There are about 900 *moai* on Easter Island. On average, they're 13 feet (4 m) high and weigh 14 tons. They're made of volcanic stone.

barrenness," Roggeveen wrote in his journal.

It was clear to Roggeveen that these few islanders could not have carved the statues, which they called *moai*. The smallest *moai* was about four feet (1.2 m) high. The very largest was 72 feet (22 m) high and weighed at least 145 tons. And there were almost 900 of the figures!

Roggeveen also wondered how these sculptures had been moved. The massive monuments were made of **volcanic** stone from **quarries** far from the coast. The islanders didn't have wheels, and there were no trees big enough to make sleds for dragging the statues. The islanders didn't even have strong vines to use as rope!

Roggeveen wrote, "We could not comprehend how it was possible that these people, who [don't have] heavy thick timber for making any machines, as well as strong ropes, had been able to erect such images."

Roggeveen saw no signs that a society capable of building such massive sculptures had ever lived on the island. Were the statues the work of an earlier and more advanced civilization?

Roggeveen left the island after five days with no answers to his questions. He called it Easter

The carved faces of the *moai* all have male features. The statues are almost identical, though some include torsos. Most of the *moai* face inward, with their backs to the ocean.

Island, in honor of the day he had arrived. It would be 200 years before scientists began to solve its mysteries.

Paradise Lost?

Fossils reveal that Easter Island had once been a very different place.

In the early 1900s, scientists began looking for answers to the questions about Easter Island. Since then, they have learned a lot about the island and the people who once lived there. Their most surprising discovery was that the island hadn't always been a treeless wasteland. In fact, for most of its history, Easter Island was a leafy paradise.

Scientists made this discovery by studying something very tiny—pollen. Pollen is a powder produced by some plants. It's made up of tiny grains. Pollen makes it possible for some plants to reproduce.

Plant scientists found fossils—or ancient remains—of pollen grains on the island. One plant's pollen does not look like the pollen from any other plant. So by examining the tiny pollen

These archeologists from the University of Chile are working on a dig on Easter Island.

fossils, scientists were able to figure out what kind of plants had once grown on the island. They were also able to tell how many of those plants had grown there.

Based on the pollen evidence, the scientists came to an amazing conclusion. For thousands of years, Easter Island had been a very green place. Many different plants and trees grew there. There were large forests of tall palm trees. Other areas were covered with grasses, ferns, and bushes.

All that plant life meant that Easter Island had been a place where a lot of people could live. There were enough natural resources to support a large population. Scientists figured out that the original settlers arrived between AD 700 and 800. They had sailed to Easter Island from other islands in the Pacific Ocean. After that, the population grew quickly. And as their numbers grew, the islanders developed a well-organized and advanced society.

Archeologists believe that the islanders began building the mysterious statues after AD 1000 and continued through the 1500s. They don't know for sure why the islanders built them, but they have several theories. One is that the statues represented chiefs whom the islanders believed were descended directly from the gods.

One thing is certain, however. There was enough food to go around, which meant that everyone didn't have to spend each day fishing or farming. The community could support a group of people whose job was to carve the giant statues.

Scientists estimate that by the 1500s, more than 9,000 people were living on the island. But 200 years later, when Roggeveen arrived, the population had shrunk to less than 2,000. The trees had disappeared, and most of the birds were gone. Nobody was building statues.

Something terrible had happened on Easter Island. It would take scientists a long time to figure out what that had been.

Moai stand watch on a beach on Easter Island. Hundreds of years ago, the Easter Island palm tree, as well as many animal species, became extinct. Since then, some palm trees have been brought back to the island.

Spelling Their Own Doom

By overusing their natural resources, the islanders caused a disaster.

A young woman and boy from Easter Island. The people who live on Easter Island are called Rapanui. They're descended from settlers who came from Polynesia, a group of islands in the Pacific Ocean.

Jared Diamond is an expert in history and biology who has studied Easter Island. He believes that "the pollen grains and [bird] bones yield a grim answer" to the question of what happened to the island.

According to Diamond, the original settlers on the island began chopping down trees as soon as they arrived. They needed wood to build houses and canoes. They also needed firewood. And they probably used logs as rollers to move the statues that they carved from the island's volcanic stone.

Soon the islanders were chopping down the trees faster than they could grow back.

What's more, there were rats that had come to the island on boats from other Polynesian islands. And these rats ran wild, feasting on palm seeds before they could sprout roots.

The pollen fossils show that by the 1400s, the Easter Island palm tree was extinct. Other trees also died out. Eventually, the forest was replaced by grass. With no trees to nest in, many of the native bird species were wiped out. That meant less food. And with no wood to build canoes, the islanders could only fish near shore. That also meant less food.

"As forest disappeared, the islanders ran out of timber and rope [made of vines] to transport and erect their statues," Diamond explains. So the statue building stopped, too. Eventually, a unique culture slowly faded away.

By the time Roggeveen arrived, the island had been treeless for a long time. The remaining islanders struggled to survive. They had little memory of their history—or of how the statues had been built and moved.

Scientists have worked hard to solve Easter Island's mysteries, and visitors today know a lot about its history. But the island still has many secrets. For instance, wooden tablets have been found with strange writing on them. The writing, which was carved into the wood using sharks' teeth, is called *rongorongo*.

Nobody has ever figured out how to read the tablets. But experts in ancient writing systems are trying to decipher them. If they succeed, will the tablets tell us more about how the islanders lived, and what they believed? Or will they just be riddles that add to the mystery of this tiny island? 24/7

These *moai* were never moved from the quarry where they were carved. They are slowly sinking into the earth.

MOVING THE MOAI
How did statue-builders move their giant sculptures?

Easter Island *moai* are huge. An average *moai* tips the scales at 14 tons—the weight of two elephants! With no wheels or machines of any kind, how did Easter Islanders move and raise these giant *moai*?

There are some wild theories. For instance, one researcher claims that boats carrying elephants were shipwrecked, and the animals ended up on the island. Then the elephants were used to pull the statues. But there is no evidence to support this theory.

Moving a Giant

Archeologists believe that the islanders dragged the statues along log rollers. In 1998, a 75-person team went to Easter Island to test that theory. They wanted to try to move a **replica** of a *moai*, using only materials that the islanders would have had. First, they put the statue on a simple wooden sled. Then they dragged the sled along log rollers. They used ropes and large wooden levers to lift and position the statue.

It was hard work, and it took a lot of people. But the experiment showed that it was possible to pull a *moai* using simple wooden tools.

Some islanders weren't convinced by the test. They believe that their ancestors used a mysterious power called *mana* to move the statues to their locations. "It wasn't done the way these archeologists did it here," says one young Easter Islander. "We believe the *moai* walked across the land, and our ancestors have celebrated it for centuries."

In 1998, archeologists tried to replicate how they believe the *moai* were dragged to the coastline and lifted into place.

LOST CIVILIZATIONS DOWNLOAD

Want to dig deeper? Here's more information about archeologists and their discoveries.

IN THIS SECTION:

▶ how archeology is making headlines today;

▶ what inspired the first archeological excavation;

▶ the tools archeologists use on the job;

▶ whether a career in archeology might be in your future.

1648
Stonehenge

A young man named John Aubrey is out hunting. He spots the prehistoric site that we now call Stonehenge. It's a circle of huge standing stones 80 miles (129 km) outside London, England. Aubrey wonders what it was, who built it, and why. He becomes one of the first to try to answer questions about ancient cultures in a scientific way.

Key Dates in Archeology

Archeologists have been digging up the past for hundreds of years.

1748 Pompeii Uncovered

A man digging in a field in southern Italy uncovers artifacts from an ancient Roman town. He has discovered the location of Pompeii (*right*), a town that was buried under a deep layer of ash when a volcano erupted in AD 79. By the 1700s, Pompeii had been largely forgotten. Soon after Pompeii's rediscovery, one of the first-ever archeological excavations began.

1940s How Old Is It?

Carbon-14 is a radioactive form of carbon found in every living thing. Scientist Willard Libby (*right*) discovers that as time passes, the carbon-14 in dead plants and animals breaks down at a certain rate. This gives archeologists a way to date—or figure out the age of—ancient objects. It is called **radiocarbon dating**.

1966 Archeology Goes High-Tech

The U.S. government launches its first satellite for observing Earth from outer space. Soon, new imaging technologies enable satellites to see underground. Some archeologists use satellite images to find evidence of ancient civilizations.

See Case #1.

1974 Army of the Dead

Workers discover the tomb of Qin Shi Huang, the first emperor of China. Qin was buried with a huge army of at least 7,000 life-size soldiers and horses made of terra cotta, a kind of clay. This army was meant to guard him in the afterlife. Qin died in about 210 BC.

2007 Artifacts Go Home

Yale University agrees to return artifacts from the Inca city Machu Picchu. A Yale explorer had excavated the objects in 1912.

In the News

Read all about it! Ancient history is the latest news.

Countries Fight Over an Ancient Queen

CAIRO, EGYPT—June 2007

Egypt wants its queen back. If the country doesn't get her, it's "scientific war." That what Zahi Hawass, Egypt's head of ancient artifacts, told *National Geographic News*. The queen in question is actually a 3,400-year-old **bust** of Nefertiti, the wife of an Egyptian pharaoh. Today, Nefertiti is on display at a museum in Berlin, Germany. She is a top tourist attraction.

The roots of the fight stretch back to 1912. That's when the painted limestone sculpture was unearthed at an archeological dig in Egypt. The German archeologists rushed the statue to their country.

Over the next decades, the Nefertiti bust became one of the most recognizable symbols of ancient Egypt. People wore Nefertiti jewelry. They decorated their homes with copies of the statue.

Queen Nefertiti was the wife of Pharaoh Amenhotep IV, who was later known as Akhenaten. Her name means "the beautiful woman has come."

Now, Egypt wants the statue back for the opening of a new museum there in 2012. But German officials say that it is too delicate to travel.

America's First Gunshot Victim Found!

LIMA, PERU—June 2007

The first person killed by a gun in the Americas was shot in the head with a musket. And that musket was fired by a Spaniard.

That's according to a new archeological find.

Peruvian archeologist Guillermo Cock recently uncovered a skull with a gunshot wound. He was excavating a cemetery outside of Lima, Peru's capital city.

Tests revealed that the victim was from the Inca period. The Incas lived in what is now Peru. Their empire was crushed by the Spanish conquerors in the 1530s.

Cock had the hole in the skull tested for iron. Why? The Spanish made their musket balls out of iron. The Incas didn't work with that metal. So if there was any trace of iron in the wound, it would prove that the man was almost certainly shot by a Spanish soldier.

A scientist found iron in the wound. Cock and his colleagues think the man was shot during the siege of Lima. In that 1536 battle, Incas fought back against the Spanish invaders.

Archeologist Guillermo Cock found this skull in a graveyard near Lima, Peru, in 2004. The hole in the top of the skull is a wound from a musket ball.

49

Tools of the Trade

Have a look at the tools and equipment you'd need on an archeological dig.

flat trowel The most important tool on many digs. Use it to carefully scrape away layer after layer of earth.

large pick Use this to loosen soil at the beginning of a job. But don't just swing away. You have to work carefully so you don't destroy important artifacts.

hand pick This small tool is good for delicate chipping or digging jobs.

household tools You'll need everyday objects like toothpicks, toothbrushes, and spoons to help uncover artifacts.

sifter screen This tool lets you sift through dirt or sand in search of tiny bits of artifacts—such as bones or pieces of broken pottery.

tape measure Want to know how tall that prehistoric statue is? You'll need a good tape measure.

sledge hammer Use this to break up large rocks at the beginning of a dig.

first aid kit Include sunscreen, bandages, antiseptic for cuts, and the medicine you'd need if you were bitten by a spider or poisonous snake.

whisk and dustpan The whisk is for brushing away dirt from your finds. The dustpan collects the dirt so you can sift it for small pieces of evidence.

51

HELP WANTED:
Archeologist

Can you picture yourself working at a dig? Meet a young archeologist who loves his job.

Q&A: LUCA CASPARIS, PHD

24/7: How did you decide to become an archeologist?

DR. LUCA CASPARIS: Between the ages of five and ten, I was really into dinosaurs. When I was 11 or 12, I realized people were a lot more interesting. On family trips, I'd drag my parents to archeological sites. I read all the time. *National Geographic* was a big influence on me, especially pictures of Mayan temples in the jungles of Mexico. By the time I was 12, I knew I wanted to be an archeologist, and I knew I wanted to work in Mexico.

Dr. Luca Casparis volunteered at the American Museum of Natural History in New York City when he was in college. He is now a research fellow there. He spends two months a year at a dig near Oaxaca, Mexico. There, he's helping to excavate Monte Albán, an ancient city that was part of the Zapotec culture.

24/7: What is the best part of your job?

DR. CASPARIS: The fieldwork. You try to come up with a good picture of what life was like and what people did. It's very slow and very detailed, and it's also very exciting.

24/7: What is the most amazing thing you've found?

DR. CASPARIS: We were excavating a temple . . . that was built of adobe [clay] bricks. In one area we found a whole set of human footprints—from people who'd built the temple 1,500 years ago! It must have rained one day while they were working and the clay got wet. It was such a direct connection to people back then.

24/7: Did you put your feet in the footprints?

DR. CASPARIS: Of course! I'm a size 12 shoe, and they were about a size 8. People were shorter back then.

24/7: Is your work ever dangerous?

DR. CASPARIS: No, Oaxaca is fairly safe. The only major danger in the area is killer bees. There are snakes, and there are tarantulas, but other than that, we've never had any problems.

24/7: Do local people work on the dig with you?

DR. CASPARIS: Yes, and it's great because they're the descendants of the people who built the city. They have a direct connection and direct knowledge. Sometimes we'll find an artifact and be puzzled by it. They'll say, "Oh, yeah. You use it for water. My grandfather had one."

24/7: What's your advice for people who are thinking about a career in archeology?

DR. CASPARIS: Read a lot and learn a foreign language. Visit archeological sites and museums. When you get to high school, volunteer on a dig. There is archeology going on in every state. Half of what I know I learned in the field. It's not just the books!

DO YOU HAVE WHAT IT TAKES?

Take this totally unscientific quiz to find out if archeology might be a good career for you.

1 Archeologists spend lots of time digging. How do you feel about getting dirty?

a) My idea of fun is a good mud fight.

b) I don't mind getting dirty if that's what it takes to get the job done.

c) Ick. Pass me the hand sanitizer.

2 Digs often take place in remote places with extreme weather and few comforts. Would you mind that?

a) If my parents let me, I'd sleep under the stars in my backyard every night.

b) I'd survive, but I'd be happy to get back home to my nice soft bed.

c) As long as there's air-conditioning, I'd be fine. And a pool, of course.

3 Archeologists sometimes discover evidence that disproves one of their theories. Can you handle it when you're wrong?

a) Finding the truth is the most important thing. I don't worry about my ego.

b) I like to be right, but if I'm wrong, I admit it.

c) I honestly don't know, since I've never been wrong.

4 Do you like learning about history and life in the past?

a) If somebody invented a time machine, I'd be first in line to use it.

b) Sure. It's fun to learn about how people used to live.

c) LOL. Next question?

5 Fieldwork involves lots of tiny details. You wouldn't want to lose track of a broken pot, for instance. Are you good with details?

a) I update my to-do list every hour. I can now check off that I completed this quiz.

b) I'm not super-organized, but I can keep track of details when I need to.

c) Why sweat the small stuff? I'm a big-picture kind of person.

YOUR SCORE

Give yourself 3 points for every "a" you chose.

Give yourself 2 points for every "b" you chose.

Give yourself 1 point for every "c" you chose.

If you got **13–15 points**, you'd probably be a good archeologist.

If you got **10–12 points**, you might be a good archeologist.

If you got **5–9 points**, you might want to look at another career!

HOW TO GET STARTED...NOW!

It's never too early to start working toward your goals.

GET AN EDUCATION

▶ Focus on your history, science, math, and foreign language classes.

▶ Look at colleges with good **anthropology** (the study of human cultures), history, and science departments.

▶ Volunteer at a museum or a dig. Not all digs are overseas. To find one nearby, go to the Web site for the organization of Archaeological Parks in the U.S. (www.uark.edu/misc/aras) Look for an archeological park in your area.

▶ Read anything you can find about archeology. There are lots of great fiction and nonfiction books about archeologists. Watch TV shows about ancient cultures. See the books and Web sites in the Resources section on pages 56–58.

▶ Graduate from high school!

NETWORK

▶ Find out about archeological groups or societies in your area. Most states have an archeological society. A librarian can help you find yours.

▶ See if you can find an archeologist who can give you advice. Start your search at a local college or museum.

GET AN INTERNSHIP

▶ Look for an internship with an archeologist at a college, museum, or government agency.

▶ Look for an internship in a science lab that analyzes archeological artifacts.

LEARN ABOUT OTHER JOBS IN THE FIELD

▶ anthropologist
▶ archeology field-worker
▶ historian
▶ lab technician

THE STATS

DAY JOB: Most archeologists are college professors. They teach, dig, and write about their work. Archeologists also work for museums, the government, or private companies.

MONEY: $30,000–$100,000, depending on training and employer.

EDUCATION: Archeologists don't have to be licensed or certified like doctors or lawyers. Experience and knowledge are most important. A few successful archeologists receive all their training on the job, but most have the following education:
▶ four years of college
▶ graduate school to receive a master's or doctorate degree

THE NUMBERS: The Archaeological Institute of America, the oldest and largest archeological organization in North America, has about 8,500 members around the world.

Resources

Looking for more information about archeology? Here are some resources you don't want to miss!

PROFESSIONAL ORGANIZATIONS

Archaeological Institute of America
www.archaeological.org
656 Beacon Street, 4th Floor
Boston, MA 02215-2006
PHONE: 617-353-9361
E-MAIL: aia@aia.bu.edu

This is America's oldest and largest organization devoted to the world of archeology.

The Canadian Archaeological Association
www.canadianarchaeology.com
Royal Saskatchewan Museum
2445 Albert Street Regina
SK S4P 3V7
PHONE: 306-787-2815
E-MAIL: president@canadian
archaeology.com

This is Canada's foremost archeological organization.

Society for American Archaeology
www.saa.org
900 Second Street NE #12
Washington, DC 20002-3560
PHONE: 202-789-8200
E-MAIL: headquarters@saa.org

The SAA is an international association dedicated to archeological research of the Americas.

Society for Historical Archaeology
www.sha.org
15245 Shady Grove Road, Ste. 130
Rockville, MD 20850
PHONE: 301-990-2454
E-MAIL: hq@sha.org

Learn more about educational and career training opportunities in archeology.

WEB SITES

The Archaeology Channel
www.archaeologychannel.org

Check out the streaming videos on this site, which showcase archeological projects from around the world.

Discovery Channel: Pompeii, the Last Day
http://dsc.discovery.com/ convergence/pompeii/pompeii. html

Read about the last day of Pompeii and learn about ongoing excavations at this site.

National Association of State Archaeologists
www.uiowa.edu/~osa/nasa/

This Web site offers a directory of links to state archeological organizations.

NOVA Online: Lost City of Arabia
www.pbs.org/wgbh/nova/ubar/

This site details the search for Ubar and offers an interview with Professor Juris Zarins.

NOVA Online: Secrets of Easter Island
www.pbs.org/wgbh/nova/easter/

Learn more about the team of archeologists who worked to unravel the mystery of Easter Island.

The Plateau: The Official Site of Dr. Zahi Hawass
http://guardians.net/hawass/

On this site, you'll learn more about Dr. Hawass and the many treasures of ancient Egypt.

The UnMuseum: The Lost Continent of Atlantis
www.unmuseum.org/atlantis.htm

This site provides various theories about Atlantis.

BOOKS

Arnold, Caroline. *Easter Island: Giant Stone Statues Tell of a Rich and Tragic Past.* New York: Clarion Books, 2000.

Caselli, Giovanni. *In Search of Troy: One Man's Quest for Homer's Fabled City.* New York: Peter Bedrick, 2001.

Kaplan, Sarah Pitt. *Pompeii: City of Ashes.* Danbury, Conn.: Children's Press, 2005.

Malone, Caroline, Nancy Stone Bernard, and Brian Fagan. *Stonehenge (Digging for the Past).* New York: Oxford University Press, 2002.

Osborne, Mary Pope. *Pompeii: Lost and Found.* New York: Knopf Books for Young Readers, 2006.

Roberts, Russell. *The Lost Continent of Atlantis.* Hockessin, Del.: Mitchell Lane Publishers, 2006.

MAGAZINES

Archaeology
www.archaeology.org

Published by the Archaeological Institute of America, it has amazing stories from around the world.

Dig!
www.digonsite.com

This is a magazine for kids published by the Archaeological Institute of America.

National Geographic
www.nationageographic.com

This magazine is full of beautiful photos and exciting stories about exploration, adventure, and world cultures.

MOVIES

The Indiana Jones Trilogy: *Raiders of the Lost Ark* (1981), *Indiana Jones and the Temple of Doom* (1984), and *Indiana Jones and the Last Crusade* (1989)
Archeologist Indiana Jones travels the world in search of treasure.

Lara Croft: Tomb Raider (2001)
Lara Croft travels the world looking for artifacts and adventure.

Legend of the Lost (1957)
Catch John Wayne in this epic adventure in the Sahara Desert.

The Mummy Trilogy: *The Mummy* (1999), *The Mummy Returns* (2001), and *The Scorpion King* (2002)
Ancient mummies come to life and threaten archeologists in 1920s Egypt.

A

allegories (AL-luh-gor-eez) *noun* fictional stories meant to teach lessons

anthropology (an-thruh-POL-uh-jee) *noun* the study of human cultures

archeology (ar-kee-OL-uh-jee) *noun* learning about past cultures by studying buildings, graves, objects, and human remains such as mummies. The word can also be spelled *archaeology*.

artifacts (ART-uh-fakts) *noun* objects made by humans, especially tools or weapons used in the past. Common artifacts found at digs include pottery and jewelry.

B

bust (BUHST) *noun* a statue of someone, usually showing the person's body from the chest up

C

caravans (KA-ruh-vanz) *noun* groups of people or vehicles that are traveling together

civilization (siv-ih-luh-ZAY-shuhn) *noun* a highly developed and organized society with its own culture and technology

concentric (kuhn-SEN-trik) *adjective* describing circles that share the same center

corrupt (kuh-RUPT) *adjective* displaying immoral behavior; often involves money, such as offering or taking bribes

D

date (dayt) *verb* to determine the age of an artifact

dig (dig) *noun* in archeology, a dig is a site that is being excavated—or dug up

E

embalming (em-BAHLM-ing) *noun* process of preserving dead bodies

evidence (EV-uh-duhnss) *noun* information or facts used to prove something or to make you believe that something is true

excavating (EK-skuh-vay-ting) *verb* digging up and recovering artifacts and other clues about people of the past

Dictionary

F

fieldwork (FEELD-wurk) *noun* work done at a dig or other archeological site

fortress (FOR-triss) *noun* a place that is strengthened against attack

frankincense (FRANK-in-sens) *noun* a kind of incense made from the sap of a tree found in Arabia and Africa

H

helm (helm) *noun* the lever or wheel that steers a ship

L

legend (LEJ-uhnd) *noun* a story passed down from earlier times that has not been proven to be true

M

moai (MOH-eye) *noun* huge human-figure statues found on Easter Island; the term is both singular and plural.

O

obsessed (uhb-SESST) *verb* fixated on one thing

P

peninsula (puh-NIN-suh-luh) *noun* a piece of land that sticks out from a larger landmass and is almost completely surrounded by water

philosopher (fuh-LOSS-uh-fur) *noun* a person who studies the nature of reality, wisdom, and knowledge

Q

quarries (KWOR-eez) *noun* places where stone, slate, and other materials are dug from the ground

R

radiocarbon dating (RAY-dee-oh KAR-bun DAY-ting) *noun* the process of figuring out how old something is by measuring the amount of radioactive carbon still present in it

replica (REP-luh-kuh) *noun* an exact copy of something

S

scorching (SKORCH-ing) *adjective* extremely hot

sediment (SED-uh-muhnt) *noun* dirt or other solid stuff that has been carried somewhere by water

submersible (suhb-MURS-uh-buhl) *noun* a small underwater craft often used for deep-sea research

T

tsunami (tsoo-NAH-mee) *noun* a very large, destructive wave caused by an underwater earthquake or volcano

V

volcanic (vol-KAN-ik) *adjective* produced by a volcano

Index

When I got the assignment to write this book about lost civilizations, I was excited. Since I love history and I love mysteries, it seemed perfect for me. Easter Island and Atlantis were the lost cities I thought of first, so I went to my laptop and started researching. I was dismayed at what I found. First, there was an article about a so-called scientist who said he'd proven that the mysterious Easter Island *moai* were built and moved by . . . drumroll please . . . aliens from outer space. Then, I happened upon an article about Atlantis. Atlantis was in the Bahamas, it said. The proof? People under hypnosis said they had spent their past lives in Atlantis, and the Bahamas was where it was. Uh-oh, I thought. Are insane people the only ones interested in lost civilizations these days?

Then I came to my senses and focused my research. It's true that the idea of lost civilizations attracts people who like to believe wild stories. But when I looked in the right places, I found lots of brilliant (and sane) people using their brainpower to unravel the mysteries of lost civilizations like Atlantis, Ubar, and Easter Island. They are archeologists, historians, and even ground-penetrating radar experts—and it really bugs them when obviously bogus, nonscientific theories get publicity!

I hope this book get you interested in doing some of your own research into lost civilizations. Before you start digging, please read these tips about how to decide whether a theory about a lost civilization is worth considering. (They're based on what I learned while I was researching.)

▶ There should be scientific evidence to support the theory. Evidence from an archeological dig is scientific. A vivid dream that someone had is not.

▶ Respected experts in archeology or history should take the theory seriously. (That doesn't mean they have to believe it.)

▶ You find information about it in reliable publications or Web sites. On the Internet, check on National Geographic (www.nationalgeographic.com) or the Web site for the science TV program *Nova* (www.pbs.org/nova).

The truth is out there. . . .

CONTENT ADVISER: Cliff Wassmann, artist and researcher, mysteriousplaces.com